COMPANIONS ON A JOURNEY:

*Walking by Faith,
Not by Sight*

Len Mac Lellan

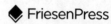 FriesenPress

Suite 300 - 990 Fort St
Victoria, BC, V8V 3K2
Canada

www.friesenpress.com

The subtitle "Walk by faith, not by sight" comes from 2 Corinthians 5:7

The pictures for this book were provided by Mary Colleen Photography

Special thanks to Angela Radzikowski for her proofreading and feedback, as well as to Mary Briand for her encouragement to publish in the first place.

ISBN
978-1-03-910868-4 (Hardcover)
978-1-03-910867-7 (Paperback)
978-1-03-910869-1 (eBook)

1. POETRY, INSPIRATION & RELIGIOUS

Distributed to the trade by The Ingram Book Company

CONTENTS HERIN

———

COMPANIONS ON A JOURNEY

There are many roads in life,
with each being neither the right nor the wrong one.
There are only the roads we take.
We can attempt to blaze our own,
set out with a fellow traveller, or maybe follow
in the footsteps of those who went before us.
Most of those you see you'll know only in passing.
But you will meet many who will want
to accompany you on your travels,
helping you or hindering along the way.
You will learn the difference.
It can be a lonely trek at times, but eventually
you will encounter a true companion.
At the crossroads ahead, if you are ready
and wise enough to recognize them,
they may join you for life.
If you choose to go on unaccompanied,
trust in your heart that you are never truly alone,
for the Helper has always been there by your side
since before you took your first steps.
Through eyes of faith, recognize the Helper's presence
guiding and protecting you
until life's lessons have been learned
and your travelling days
have slowed to completion.

DEDICATION

This book is dedicated to my family,
to past and present companions
who have shared a common journey,
and to St. Rita's Parish
to whom the proceeds
of this book will be going
to help pay for
the new gathering centre.

SOJOURNS HOME

CAIRNS OF HOPE

Deep in tuition loans debt,
I sought a secluded beach by the sea
to be alone with God.
In solemnity and sincerity, I pleaded,
"I need a teaching job,"
as I heaved one prayer stone after another
toward the heavens
and clumsily down upon the others.
Wishing to turn stones into bread,
I put my heart and straining back
into raw, simple prayers.
"Give me courage," as I muscled
large lopsided boulders onto the pile.
"Guide me," as I turned
and stumbled down the beach for more.
With my head throbbing
and my arms and belly chaffed and stinging,
I knew I had no more to give
as I stood in silence among the trinity
of stone cairns upon the seashore.
With all my vigour and prayers spent,
I washed in the changing tide
before making my way home
to await His reply.

LEAVING

My papa confided in me that every time
he left Nana and their children behind
to work away in Newfoundland or Ontario,
his tears fell like a blinding rain,

knowing it would be months before
he would be able to return home.

The first time I left Cape Breton to teach in the west
I was a single man, yet I too struggled
to see the road through my tears.
Yet in the years to follow,
my eyes were opened to God's plan,
including a job, home, and a family.

Like Atlantic salmon, we may return one day,
leaving this sea of wheat to navigate
our way back to my home by the river.
Just to have the pattern repeated
when our children are grown up
and need to find work in the west.
It will be their turn to dry their eyes
as they pull out of the driveway,
praying for the courage to go,
while pushing from their minds
every reason to stay.

LEAVING AND THE LEFT

It's never easy to leave
with prolonged solemn goodbyes,
swift parting hugs, and it's done
before yonder rising sun
brings to light moist woeful eyes
and a grieved heart on my sleeve.

To disconnect heart and mind,
I focused on roads ahead,
hence bypassed forecasted pain

or what felt like tepid rain
clouding the words left unsaid
to family left behind.

There was solace in the fact
brief returns could be arranged
in a year or maybe more,
and I'd walk through kindred door
like nothing had ever changed,
though I'd know it's just an act.

As they surely saw in me
one different standing there
after the passage of time,
altered features and the mind,
yet to say we do not dare
as each pretends not to see.

That is the price to be paid
when loved ones at home are left
for the young's personal gain,
while nothing remains the same
and regret pervades the guest
knowing that he cannot stay.

I AND EVERYTHING
(FOR MY WIFE)

I wish her embrace was mine
her who I'm drawn to like no other
that her touch would be upon me
against me her soft skin pressed
my neck warming beneath her breath
her calming words in close ear

my lips so smooth on her cheek
in her hair my gentle caress.

My thoughts are in wonderment of her
spinning my mind beyond reason
stirring my essence with her presence
lighting the pale world before me
my eyes are cast in admiration
awestruck by this yonder young vision
her of the black hair and dark eyes
simple beauty beyond imagination.

My soul reaches out in tenderness
giving of myself to win her favour
a mere glance of her delicate features
fills my heart with drumming elation
what I wouldn't offer to bring
hasn't yet been made or spoke of
I know with blissful certainty
to her I'd give I and everything.

DIDN'T FEEL LIKE CHRISTMAS

———

I felt the December nip in the air,
saw red and green fashions kids did wear,
as parents bought gifts without a care,
yet it didn't feel like Christmas.

The final day of school brought smiles and cheer,
went home to delight in junk food and beer;
not driving to the airport felt so weird,
yet it didn't feel like Christmas.

With two vacation weeks to have a ball,
finished shopping at the busy mall,

the absence of snow made it feel like fall,
yet it didn't feel like Christmas.

Sang at midnight Mass those carols of glee,
gave and received gifts from under the tree,
celebrated until quarter to three,
yet it didn't feel like Christmas.

A few days before my work would begin,
not knowing whether to frown or grin,
I was left to balance losses with wins,
since it didn't feel like Christmas.

We saved some money by not flying home,
exchanged holiday greetings on the phone,
didn't know when I had felt so alone,
since it didn't feel like Christmas.

From family back home we were apart,
so we blocked our tears and deceived our hearts.
My wife carried me through this trying time,
since the pains of longing weren't solely mine.
Over a short time learned a lesson tall,
my first Christmas from home
didn't seem like Christmas at all.

GREATEST GIFT

I look up to my dad in the same way I did as a boy,
as a man of strength, courage, and craftsmanship.
I suppose in my eyes he'll never change.
When I finally decided to settle down
in Valleyview, Alberta, with my wife-to-be,
we looked at the houses that were available.
When we didn't find what we were looking for,

I asked my dad if he could come out with mom
to build us an eastern style home in the west.
Being sixty years old at the time,
he had every right or reason to turn us down,
but he didn't. He just said, "I suppose."
So I bought a piece of land and we picked out
a house blueprint that we liked.
Dad packed his truck with carpentry tools
and sent it by train to Edmonton.
We picked Mom and Dad up at the airport,
and the truck at the CN depot,
before driving north to Valleyview,
where we stayed at my apartment
just a short drive from our lot.
From that point on, my memories fast forward,
with the business of clearing the trees, pouring footings,
spreading gravel, preparing forms,
pouring the basement, installing weeping tile,
erecting pony walls, decking joists, framing walls,
roofing rafters, shingling and tarring, insulating,
dry walling, sanding, painting, siding,
and a thousand other steps
that my father knew how to do well.
The photographs of those stages of the construction
captured just how beautiful the process really was.
My dad and mom working side by side
will always be the most enduring memory.
"It was fun," my mother still says
when she speaks of those days
working as one under the sun.

There hasn't been a day since its completion
that my wife and I haven't felt extremely blessed
for the time we shared, for the home we built,

for the neighbours who helped us,
and for my parents who made it all possible.
I look around often at the workmanship
and I fondly remember them
as they measured, sawed, and hammered
the pieces of our beloved home together.
Every corner is a monument to their efforts.

Before my dad left to go back east,
he turned and said to me, "Take care of it."
I want you to know, Dad, that we have,
this being the last house you ever built,
and the greatest gift of love
a son could ever receive.

THE HORSE TRAILER

During those months of our home construction,
when the rainstorm or mealtime rumbles were heard,
my fiancé, father, mother, and I would retreat
into the cozy confines of the horse trailer.
Lent to us by thoughtful neighbours,
this aluminum enclosure shielded our tools,
materials, and us from the summer sun, wind, and rain.
Sitting on stacked two by fours on either side,
it also served as a makeshift galley,
where we doled out
chicken sandwiches wrapped in cellophane,
juice boxes, granola bars, and apples from the cooler.
For dessert, hearty helpings of laughter
were shared around those rustic quarters,
helping to lift us out of the fatigue, sweat, and mud.
Our little family, huddled together
in hope, hospitality, and humour,

thankful for our stable of sorts,
with no want or need of an inn.

ARRIVAL HOME

I feel extremely fortunate to have
the life that I do. To live in a warm home
with an unselfish wife, who tends to the needs
of our family with love, patience and devotion.
To have a mother-in-law who sees to the making
of not just a breakfast, but my favourite one
each early morning. To pick up my lunch
that has been prepared with capable hands
as I gaze for fleeting moments into the eyes
and smiling face of our daughter.
As I walk out the door I thank God
for the blessings in my life.
It is enough to get me through
even a long, unpleasant day,
joyfully aware that there will be
supper and my loving family
awaiting my arrival.

91

MY HEROINE

Hurtling like a comet through space,
I sat tensely in the cockpit
as blurred supernovas by us flashed.
For what seemed like light years,
my vision tunnelled
into the coal black night ahead
until our shuttle docked
near the station entrance.

Soon there would be much pushing,
panting, vocalizing, and bleeding
before this close encounter
of the most unforgettable kind would be over.
Yet this was no science fiction
as I watched with wonder and amazement
as my son and daughter came into the world.
In the relative calm that followed,
I looked down in awe
at Maureen's relieved and tired face
and saw a semblance of
Mother Mary, Helen of Troy,
and Boudicca, the warrior queen,
encompassed all into one woman:
my wife, my heroine.

OUR CHILDREN

They're young only once.
Play with them, double the fun.
You'll be twice the man.

DADDY'S WORLD

Saturday mornings were always fun with our children.
From under a roomy bed sheet I would commence singing,
"Daddy's world, Daddy's world, it's the best in Daddy's world."
Of course, the kids would try to find a way in,
yanking on the sheet edges that I was struggling to hold down.
Eventually heads would appear toward the foot of the bed,
and they would crawl up. Laughing, I'd ask, "How did you get in?"
"I found the key," they would say, as I began tickling them.
Soon I'd be alone again undercover, singing,

"Daddy's world, Daddy's world, it's the best, in Daddy's world,"
whereupon they would renew the search for a different way in,
because they knew, as I did,
it was always the best
in Daddy's world.

THE STROLLER

As much as I enjoy taking photographs,
there are times when I prefer
to preserve the essence of a moment
by pouring it out onto a page
to be later sipped and savoured
like a mellow homemade wine.
Like the day of my wife's yard sale,
watching a red truck carry away
Alexis' orange baby stroller,
tearing at my heart strings as it went,
knowing my days behind it
had all been so swiftly spent.
Every drop of emotion
I squeezed from simmering memories
were stirred round with my pen,
yielding a bitter sweet blend,
tasting more intense
than would have ever been possible
at any other moment
than this.

FAREWELL MR. ROGERS

The day I heard of the passing
of the great singer-storyteller Kenny Rogers,

it wasn't enough for me to feel sad and sentimental.
I wanted to voice my gratitude for sharing with us
his passionate and authentic music "Through the Years."
As I readied to vacuum the basement,
I cranked the volume on one of his CDs,
and instantaneously the rug became my stage,
the vacuum nozzle my microphone, and our three kids
my adoring fans. First I was The Gambler,
teaching Allan "When to hold 'em" and "When to fold 'em,"
Anna grew into my Lady, and I her "Knight in shining armour,"
and Alexis became Ruby as I begged her
not to "Take her love to town."
The kids had no clue what I was going through,
but they were thoroughly entertained by my tribute.
As I brought my impromptu show to a close
I felt joyful, as if Lucille had come home for good,
the crops were in, the children were fed,
cowards had turned into heroes,
islands in the stream had been bridged,
and your many good works here Kenny
had all been accomplished.

DO YOU WANT TO PLAY, DADDY?

It is as if I am watching myself play as a boy,
with sounds, incomplete conversations,
and fun-filled actions. With scarce room
within the closed ranks of his sisters,
my young son is left with few playmates
with which to occupy his mind.
In times like this, I suppose he would feel
utterly lonely if it wasn't for
his acute six-year-old imagination,

plus he has me.
With that in mind, I must go,
for my son has asked me to come play,
and the little boy inside of me
aches to join him.

THE TEA PARTY

From the back of her closet, my daughter pulled out
a children's tea set that had never been played with before.
As the box was being opened for the first time,
I could see our kids examining each piece carefully,
admiring the "Three Bear" illustrations
that appeared on each tiny plate, teacup, and teapot.
As they delicately laid them out on a little wooden table,
someone cried out, "Let's have a tea party!"
and the others retorted with a resounding, "Yeah!"
They began to organize the dishes atop a towel tablecloth,
as root beer, with sugar and milk added, became hot tea,
and bread and apple slices became the delectable main courses.
My wife and I watched them play out their tea party
as they sat comfortably in their little wooden chairs,
laughing as they shared all that they prepared.
They brought over some tea for us to sample
that wasn't too hot or too cold. It was just right!
When the guests were ready to depart, my son said,
"Can we play this every night?" "Sure," I said,
thinking how nice it was to see them in this light,
serving each other rather than being served,
sharing the food and drinks they had prepared,
and playing the hospitable host to their siblings.
It was heartwarming to watch them act so maturely
and considerately in each other's company,

even if the cordial interaction lasted only until
this poem had drawn to a close.

WINTER WALK

Hoar-frosted twigs pass
as my son's hand warms in mine.
Beauty abounds here.

FORTY-NINE AND COUNTING

This is the last day before I turn fifty.
As I walked with my wife, we talked
about which decade past was the most memorable,
but I was never able to decide.
The first ten years I learned
to read, spell, and how to be kind.
In my teen years, I left home to learn
life lessons in cadet camp and later in university.
In my twenties, I finished my degrees
and ventured west to teach.
In my thirties, I found a reason to build a home
and married my wife.
In my forties, I witnessed the birth of our children
and the launch of my first book.
Not being able to put my finger
on which decade was my most memorable,
I concluded optimistically that it would likely be
the one that was about to begin.
That is assuming I will be wiser and more patient,
trusting that the road God had prepared for us
would take us to where we needed to go next.

HALF A CENTURY

Fifty is just a number,
but what made it extraordinary
was the emotion I felt on my birthday.
With the kids' urging, I left our bedroom and found
our home decorated with my colourful tie collection.
There was a birthday banner with my face on it,
brought back from the Philippines
by my thoughtful mother-in-law.
There was a birthday cheesecake with a candle,
and three beautiful handmade cards from our children.
After I sat at the kitchen table,
my wife read and played birthday greetings
and I was moved deeply by the outpouring
of such kind and meaningful words.
Not getting out or having people over this year
didn't seem to matter as much,
since I received heartfelt gifts
of appreciation and love.
I don't think
I could have asked for more.

TONING IT DOWN

There have been long days like today,
when my impatience and fatigue have tinged
my attitude's lighter tones,
resulting in unintentional emotional shades.
I don't remember what I said to my son
that caused him to cry, but I knew
I should have said it in a better way.
When I felt the time was right, I sat on his bed

and asked him why he was crying.
He said, "You hurt my heart."
I felt his words instantaneously in my own
and knew he was right.
After a heart-to-heart talk and a hug,
I apologized to Allan for my unnecessary tone
and for hurting his feelings.
Soon all was right again
and I walked away realizing
it was such a small amount of time and effort
for an impatient father to pay
so his own son's heart could be mended.
Thus two hearts were healed
for the price of one.

CLOUDS

They hug the ground on fall mornings,
transforming lowland expanses
into mysterious inland seas
dotted with tranquil treed islands,
while some adorn loftier realms
with fine white brush strokes
on cosmic cobalt canvases.
Many congregate above the plains,
adrift like lofty icebergs of cotton
across deep blue titanic skies,
while others loom dark and low,
mopping the dusty fields and forests
with countless drenching tentacles.
Yet no clouds are so beautiful to me
as those billowy stepping stones below,
wafting by my airplane window

in giant easterly leaps,
leading me home.

LETTING GO

We hung on with our fingernails
against all hope and reason until now,
and with the click of the mouse
our high hopes of a vacation back home
have been brought down in flames.
I know we are not alone in this
since smoldering holiday wreckage
similar to our own,
can be spotted everywhere I look.
Some may not understand
but the thought of getting back east
sees us through the long winter months,
promising spiritual rejuvenation
through family reconnection.
But in the end, risks were too high,
and the quarantine too long.
Now we'll have to make the best of it.
So if you'll excuse me,
I need to go tell the kids.

VISION OF HOME

I dreamt I was back east last night,
for through my window I could see
a well-known view of grass and trees
clearly perceived within mind's sight.

In the thick of those boyhood scenes,
I believed I was really home,
just to waken, chafed to the bone,
with nothing but distance between.

ENCOURAGEMENT

As I readied for bed, I heard Allan say,
"Want me to show you how wiggly my tooth is?"
I bent down to look, and he proudly wiggled
one of his front top teeth back and forth with his finger.
"I've been working on it," he said,
looking so wide-eyed and serious.
"You know what you're doing," I said.
"You can handle that,"
and he was soon fast asleep.

Before our school relaunch, I called my mother,
since she'd taught grade five for many years.
I told her about how many students I had
but mostly dwelled on the new challenges that stood
between Covid-19 and the classroom.
Hearing the seriousness and concern in my voice,
she reassured me,
"You know what you're doing. You can handle it,"
and with that my anxiety lifted.
I guess all a son really needs
is a little encouragement.

SEASONAL CHANGE

Window tap above.
Saw my daughter smile and wave
as winter turned spring.

GRANDMA LUCY

After living with us for over seven years,
my mother-in-law, Lucy, moved out
to live with my sister-in-law's family.
During our time together, we looked after her
and she looked after us.
Like strong silken thread,
she helped to strengthen our family fabric
with her homemade Asian cuisine,
her loyal and compassionate nature,
as well as her loving and gentle ways.
We will miss her dearly, and not only that,
I've noticed since her departure
that not only has our world gotten a little bit smaller,
but our skies have dimmed without her bright smile,
and the climate has cooled considerably
in the absence of her warm heart.
Even the summer flowers have begun to wilt.
But despite the lack of sunshine,
I have seen growth in me -
as I find myself cooking, serving meals,
doing the dishes, and folding the laundry
more than I ever did before.
It could be true what they say:
that with the setting of the sun,
another will surely rise.

ANNIVERSARY

I am humbled by the significance of this day.
Fourteen years ago my wife and I stood together
and promised to share our journey of a lifetime.
Of all the many roads in life to follow,
ours has been one of ups and downs
as we explore the challenges
of parenthood, careers, and community life.
Our feet have felt both bliss and blisters
as we made our way through a triathlon
of stress, fatigue, and compromise
by sharing the load together.
In situations that seemed beyond our control,
we learned to trust in God and ourselves
to get us back on track.
I see this day less a victory march
after years with the same woman
but more a time of simple appreciation.
When God matched this old weary wanderer
with an energetic travelling partner
who helped me reach those life destinations
that would have been impossible to find alone.
I pray for the strength and wisdom
to keep moving in the right direction
along life's hidden and challenging pathways.

COVID-19 SHUFFLE

CLOSING THE DISTANCE

———

As Covid-19 spreads steadily it has forced the world apart.
The silver lining is that I find myself with an abundance
of quality time to spend with my family.
Since the switch to daylight saving,
my daughter and I have embraced the extra hour
by cross-country skiing atop the newly fallen snow.
Meandering deer trails crisscross ahead of us
creating the illusion of a patchwork quilt
blanketing the floor of the leafless forest.
Like peace offerings, we leave gifts of carrots, apples, pears,
or, if the deer are lucky, giant strawberries
smuggled from the refrigerator.
Eventually the deer stop bounding away
and instead watch us with curiosity.
The silence in those moments is almost magical.
I look forward to every opportunity to be brought closer
to my daughter and the deer of the forest
during this most opportune time
of physical distancing.

BRIDGES

(TO HANNAH KNOWLES)

———

Recently I learned two important lessons.
My first lesson was learning to reach out digitally
to teach my students who are at home during the outbreak.
I surprised myself and others because I was not normally
one to utilize online technology for education's sake.
I have always considered myself a traditional stand-up teacher
but have made the transition, by opening up to learning
something new from a younger teacher on our staff.

LEN MAC LELLAN

This was lesson two.
Being older and experienced, my ego had me convinced
that I did not have much more to learn,
especially from one so new to the profession.
I soon found out how much useful knowledge she possessed.
I merely humbled myself and allowed her to show me
how to open cyber doors so my students could enter.
It was like a new awakening for me and I am so appreciative.
I am a better teacher because of her.

HAPPY SIXTH BIRTHDAY!

Our twins' birthday is here
and we ease into the celebration.
There are balloons, a birthday banner,
and a modest number of cards and gifts to open.
Friends watch from their iPad screens
as Allan and Anna blow out
six candles on their ice cream cake.
As we settle down in our living room,
there is singing, smiles, and laughter.
It isn't long before the party is over
and I am left feeling contented
that my family is happy, healthy, and safe.
In cautious times such as these
there can be no better gifts.

SOCIAL DISTANCING

In these days of social distancing,
my family and I try to make the best
of this stressful and isolating time.
I especially like letting my inner child out

to play with our children.
Whenever I find my patience wearing thin,
I try not to let the puddles beside the bathtub,
the globs of toothpaste in the sink,
or the toys under my feet bother me.
It isn't always easy to be tolerant
when your mental health is regularly tested,
but my faith calms me like a patient whisper,
assuring me that this difficult time shall pass.
It is my hope that when my family and I
look back on this phase of our lives,
we will remember it not for its frustrations
but rather for how well we treated each other
as we treaded the calm waters together
in the safe harbour of home.

THOUGHTS IN PASSING

He recognizes the faces
though rarely recalls the names,
but it doesn't really matter
since he treats each one the same.
With a gentle wave or slight nod
he offers a welcome smile,
or a pause for conversation
for maybe a little while.
Life's too short to remain distant
as neighbors go striding by,
so take a moment to look up
if only to whisper "Hi."

FROM DARKNESS TO LIGHT

Through winter, I came to appreciate the spring.
Through sickness, I came to appreciate good health.
Through loneliness, I came to appreciate family.
Through fear, I came to appreciate faith.
Through sinfulness, I came to appreciate forgiveness.
Through failure, I came to appreciate determination.
Through conflict, I came to appreciate acceptance.
Through death, I came to appreciate the living.
It is because of life's miseries and unpleasantries
that I've come to appreciate all the good in my life.
Like my discerning eyes opening
after the dark.

CANADA GOOSE EXPRESS

As if on time, I see them departing,
speeding away before cold winter's frost.
Like passengers on a runaway train,
following bearings to far southern stops.

Riding the rails below low clouds lying,
their calls above town are eerily lost.
V after V I count past a thousand,
successions of cars one hundred across.

Winged carriages away from me pulling,
as if from a station watching them go.
They leave together for warmer places,
leaving me lonesome, awaiting the snow.

TO CROSS-COUNTRY SKI

———

Cross-country skiing alone
rarely feels like a solitary experience,
with a calm cloud cluster as company
or the smiling sun over your shoulder.
Fresh breezes brush your cheek
as twigs and branches offer
subtle waves as you go by.
Countless multi-coloured eyes
in the guise of snow crystals
shimmer and wink in your direction.
Chatty feathered friends
always sing their favourite tunes
as the snow below you effortlessly supports
the weight of all your worries.
With the human world left far behind,
your heartbeat falls into rhythm
with the soft swishing of a peaceful trail.
Yes, I would agree,
skiing is anything but lonely.

SLEDDING

———

Having to stay close to home during our Easter break,
I do not know what we would have done
were it not for the tobogganing hill.
From its heights we were free to visually travel
across distant treetop expanses,
felt our children's excitement
as they settled into place on the sled,
and heard their laughter cascade
down the smooth slippery slope.

After days of moving bottom to top, top to bottom,
we never reached a destination during our entire time off.
But that's all right, since sledding is really only about
the thrilling journey.

TIES THAT BIND

It doesn't matter what your age is,
one of the best ways to form relationships
is through shared similar interests.
It's the commonality of it.
Some people work out, play card games
or team sports, visit together,
or take their child out for a ski.
It was singing in the church choir
that brought my wife and me together.
Bonds are formed through shared experience.
Of course, coming together in such a way
does not guarantee a close friendship.
Nevertheless, more than anything,
it is the common threads that bind.

CRIB

I played cards in the staffroom for twenty-four years,
but our pastime has been lost in the shuffle since Covid.
It was a type of brotherhood, and crib was our game.
Except for a little counting, it gave rest and balance
to the structure and seriousness of the day.
I took solace in knowing that each recess
there was someone waiting to share
a fun diversion we enjoyed in common.
Cards made us proficient at making the best

of what we have little control of,
as we played out whatever was dealt to us
with quiet acceptance,
and no matter how bad our luck got
we were determined to never give in.
Win or lose, we were there for each other.

WHEN THE SPRING LEAVES FELL
(TO THE RESIDENTS OF NOVA SCOTIA)

Fall grass will wither upon wide open prairies,
as wilted flowers fall upon pastoral scenes.
Weary poplars cast off brownish-orange canopies
before drifting off to wintery spring dreams.

One never expects to hear of spring leaves falling
like they did in the east, while fresh and newly green.
The forests between us fell woefully silent,
like a reverent calm before the gale force screams.

Amid this storm, a country now stands beside you,
like steadfast oaks, for beloved brethren to lean.
You are not alone in your sorrowful season
as we pray together for the healing sunbeams.

For your beautiful foliage, too early fallen,
the good Gardener will be there to gently glean.
He will bring them to grow upon peaceful meadows,
to fall no more in His placid garden, unseen.

BUZZ CUT

A voracious insect buzzes swaths
across the smooth headlands above

as clumps of scrawny fir tumble down the cape
like tangled grey-brown thickets,
droning my mind into dormancy
and easing my body into timeless depths.
Suddenly, my consciousness is yanked
back to the bright surface,
and with my eyelids still half-closed,
I rub the clear cut stubble with a surveyor's hand,
regretting why something so relaxing
had ended so quickly,
wishing that I only
had more to give.

LAST DAY

It is the last day of online learning with my class.
Normally, I'd feel relief and joy
knowing that the school year is over.
Today, however, I feel a tinge of sadness
after saying goodbye on a computer screen.
During this Covid-19 crisis,
I understand it was necessary to physically distance,
since our actions contained the spread
and probably saved lives.
But using technology has so many limitations
and has left me with a lesser sense
of personal connection with my students.
Building relationships and creating memories
is an essential part of being a teacher.
It is those face-to-face, personal connections
that will often endure far into the future,
beyond many of the skills and knowledge
that I was hired to teach my students.

Cherished memories, after all, are among
the few treasured intangibles taken
when it's time for us to go.

WIND AND SEA
(INSPIRED BY ALLAN MAC LELLAN)

Wind and sea, wind and sea, all I want is wind and sea.
Arriving amid pain and glee, bouncing upon each bended knee,
splashing around with family, when I first knew of wind and sea.
Wind and sea, wind and sea, all I want is wind and sea.
I grew to pursue my own needs, seeking praise, glory, small trophies,
strutting my youthful vanity, along the shore of wind and sea.
Wind and sea, wind and sea, all I want is wind and sea.
I claimed my part of earth and tree, bartering time to make money,
hoarding effects and property, missing the peace of wind and sea.
Wind and sea, wind and sea, all I want is wind and sea.
Decades rush by when life's busy, tap our strength and vitality,
suppose good health will always be, unchanging like the wind and sea.
Wind and sea, wind and sea, all I want is wind and sea.
When all seems lost for he or she, remember what is given free,
eternal gifts in front of me, my timeless friends of wind and sea.
Wind and sea, wind and sea, all I want is wind and sea.

WHEN TIME STANDS STILL

On hot summer days when the river is low,
I step back in time millions of years ago
to walk ocean beds under the Bear Paw Sea
while holding my breath, hoping only to see
uncoiled ammonites like sparkling opal gems
or a bivalve cast among crossed rocky stems.

Newly found relics never fail to surprise,
being the first man to spot with eager eyes
natural treasures tumbled from silty banks;
so to you, cretaceous fossils, I give thanks,
for the days spent with you, alone with my thoughts,
brought peace to my time whenever it was sought.

FLEETING SUMMER MORNING

There are chicks hidden somewhere
in the direction of my wife's garden
just beyond our wooden fence.
Lying in bed we hear them:
"Tweet, tweet. Tweet, tweet, tweet,"
and again as we play crib in the evening.
Their sharp, unrelenting peeps
have brought me to watch
through the screen window.
Mama bird eyes me silently from our gate post,
her beak crammed with a lively breakfast
before disappearing into the leafy arms
of a tight knit family of alders.
I could walk over to find the nest,
but I am content to listen from a distance
as the doting mother is welcomed home by her young.
Closing my eyes, I breathe in the cool dawn
and hold her deeply, not willing to surrender
such sumptuous summer moments
before they slowly slip away
like a reluctant morning sigh.

31|

MADE IN THE SHADE

————

Our kids in a line biking down the road,
stopping at signs then steady as she goes.
Travelling so fast with no training wheels,
coasting down through town is how freedom feels.
When we turn around and head back uphill,
complaints start to swirl with a long way still.
No need to worry, since we have it made
sipping cold water in the shade, shade, shade!

JOHNSON PARK

————

On the hottest day of the summer
I sit on a folding chair in the shallows
of a clear, cool stream tickling
past my ankles and toes,
like a refreshing fountain of youth.
Pushing my heels into fine soft sand,
they find refuge and rest
in the soothing palms of Mother Earth,
as mercy descends from
shady poplar leaf canopies
and mossy spruce branches above.
Peacefulness abounds here,
simply by watching children float down
this perpetual river of dreams
upon inflatable unicorns,
a rocket ship, and giant pineapples.
As we turn for home at the end of a restful day,
a final parting gift is found
on a warm evening breeze
as I overhear my daughter, Anna, say,

"I had so much fun,
I forgot about the Coronavirus."

THROUGH THEIR EYES

It is not just the sparkling sea, the rolling highlands,
or my eastern relations I'll miss most this August.
What hurts is not being able to enjoy
these people and places through my children's eyes
as they jump crashing waves on a sandy beach,
or defend their crumbling castle walls
from an impending tide,
or bask in a seaside sunset together.
Finding joy in their joy is what I'll miss most
or that feeling of happiness that finds me
as I watch them blossom like flowers
in the warm arms of summer
after a long, withering
western winter.

33|

MOUNTAIN B & B

Through this second storey window
it appears all nature has failed to rise
as rain falls in perfect vertical lines
between this wilderness collage of misty greens
and the jagged mountain ridges beyond.

Clouds slowly shift in varying shades
in contrast to the restful spruce and pine
across and below me,
leaning in still and enviable slumber,

oblivious to the waking calls
of the crow and squirrel.

Softly intermingled with the spitter-spatter
of a fresh morning shower
is the familiar pitter-patter of little feet
ascending the hewn log staircase
as I ready myself to shake off
these final droplets of quiet solitude
and happily usher in
the beginning of a new day.

JOHN DAN MAC LELLAN

———

Jesse O'Brien was home atop
River Denys Mountain, Cape Breton,
looking after her sick grandson,
John Dan Mac Lellan.
The one-and-a-half-year-old
was suffering from diphtheria,
a bacterial infection most likely
brought home by one of the men
working at the Marble Mountain Quarry.

The rooster got into Jesse's home that day,
and this blond-haired, blue-eyed toddler
got after it and chased it outside.
John Dan walked over to his grandmother,
raised his arms for her to pick him up
and passed away in her lap.

Although my Great Uncle John Dan
was laid to rest almost 130 years ago,
I find myself pondering about him

as my children and I ready for school.
Viruses can be like that:
spread unintentionally to the innocent
with uncertain consequences.
My teacher's heart skips a beat
just thinking about how grave
unintentional consequences
can really be.

GOING BACK

There are always assumed risks to any job,
and some can be deadly.
My Great Uncle Allan Mac Lellan
died in October, 1908, after lighting a fuse
that had been cut too short
at the Marble Mountain Quarry,
and Great Uncle L/Cpl Murdock Mac Donald
died in October of 1944
after moving a booby trapped gate in Holland.

School teaching wouldn't be considered
among the most dangerous jobs in the world,
but it too has its risks.
My mother, Gloria Mac Lellan,
lost half of her first year teaching
after contracting rheumatic fever
from one of her students in 1966.

We as a staff have prepared
for the return to the classroom
and we will implement the new safety procedures
and get the job done well.
I pray for the courage to come to work each day

and for students, staff, and parents to stay healthy.
May fear not prevent us
from performing our important ministry
in this world of unpredictability.
With so much out of our control,
I trust firmly in my colleagues and in God
that everything will work out okay.

SEPTEMBER PRAYER

Over many years of teaching,
I've seen children endure suffering
when the adults around them
hurt themselves and others.
Again, my path and the paths
of a new batch of youngsters
have merged together.
God, provider and planner,
inspire me for another year
so I may be an inspiration for them.
Help me to find peacefulness within
so that they may know Your calm
and peaceful ways in my classroom.
Allow my faith to grow
so I may instill in my students
trust in the everlasting love and mercy
that You have for us all.

HORSES

I miss seeing the horses up on the yonder hill.
Chasing one another or calmly standing still.
Or slowly grazing onward through grasses side by side.

Looking up to see me as I went striding by.
Not far from work I saw them through frost and summer too.
Now pastures lie empty, shading my glad heart blue.
To me you were a lesson when I was feeling down.
Whispered, "Just keep going," yet never made a sound.

SILENT NIGHTS

Crimson sacrificial lights
on our island self-imposed
flickered from our windows bright,
during lonesome silent nights
like a warming hopeful glow.
Holy families we are
amid helpless circumstance,
loving neighbours from afar,
wishing on that Christmas star
for a close to the distance.
Wise men will arrive one day
with gifts more precious than gold,
and in the future we'll say,
we sacrificed many ways
for the sake of young and old.
For masked shepherds all are we
watching over other's folds,
so around next year's tree,
safe our families will be
to hear His story retold.

HOLDING IT TOGETHER

With the sun and stillness promising ideal conditions
our children and I ventured out beneath an inviting blue sky.

What began as an afternoon of tobogganing soon developed
into a playful construction project. The kids began by prying up
hefty helpings of crusty snow at the bottom of the hill
and were standing them on end. I joined their engineering endeavor
by repurposing the toboggans to transport unwieldy blocks
from our snowbank quarry to the building site. Leaning one heavy piece
against another, sturdy looking sections soon stood in the balance.
Smaller slabs were propped against the wobbly walls by the kids
for further reinforcement. What first resembled an ancient
megalithic formation, slowly evolved into a humble snow fortress.

With one room complete, the kids withdrew for the thrills
of the slippery slope, yet my inner child carried on
with extending and strengthening the zigzagging partitions.
Like a seasoned snow mason, I found joy and calm
with each hunk of snow I sliced, shaped and fit into place.

When my wife arrived, we worked side by side as partners and playmates.
Covid clouds seemed to scatter as we patted snow into gaps
and smoothened rough patches with utmost care.
Once the task was completed we stood back and brushed off the dust.
With a measure of satisfaction we scanned the misshapen walls
and thought the haphazard design to be almost reminiscent
of the months spent rebuilding a new sense of normalcy.
Far from perfect, there was no need to fix a thing.
We had tried our best and had little left
but sincere gratitude for the hands
that helped hold it all together.

TREKKING THE ROAD WITHIN

TO WRITE

Though the print is black upon this page,
do not think my thoughts dark.
Between the protective covers of this book
I will let my thoughts shine again.
Not to sparkle, but to fulfill.
I have much to express,
and the time and the place is now.
I'd like to say that I do this for you,
but in truth I write for no one
but the possessor of this pen,
the holder of these thoughts,
the constant and indispensable
spirit within.

ONE STEP AT A TIME

Walking has taken my mind many places.
Striding on our treadmill, for instance,
gives me an opportunity to imagine things
that I normally wouldn't have time to think about,
like poetry ideas for this book.
As a boy, I would often use my mind's eye
in much the same way as I mowed the grass
or delivered *Chronicle Herald* newspapers
in the early hours before school.
It was my imagination that allowed me
to mentally escape the monotony
of fatigue, temperature, or mosquitos
by using the time to visualize
about what made me happy
and about the man I wanted to be.

When I look back, it is really amazing
just how far my footsteps have taken me.

REFINER'S FIRE

I once was young, but now my age is great;
had thick hair on my head, but not of late.
I struggled in school, but now I teach things;
was so quiet in our church, but now I sing.
I once dreaded big words but now read well;
disdain for writing changed, as you can tell.
I grew up in the east but now dwell west;
had first not a home but now have a nest.
I owed for student loans, but now I'm fine;
once struggled finding love, but now it's mine.
Things change, and it isn't always easy
as life prepares us for our ministry.
From our greatest hurts comes our greatest gifts;
weakness becomes strength when He gives a lift.
God will be there to lend a helping hand,
to prepare us to serve our fellow man.

SHARED VISIONS

Don't give up and we will see
small glimpses of God's vision.
Divine plans for you and me,
to fulfill all that we can be
on our sacred life missions.

CERTAINTY

Sometimes I take for granted that our lives
will always stay the same
as we navigate along the road of life.
When things get too busy, I seldom stop
to view all the subtle changes within my family.
Transformations come to finer focus
only after developing pictures from our camera
and I take a moment to look at how different
we are now as compared to then.

Part of me is resistant to change
and is not ready to accept that I won't always have
the same good things in my life,
like my health, my job, money,
an energetic wife, young children,
and my mom and dad just a phone call away.
I like to assume these situations and people
are perpetual because I take comfort
in the certainty it offers me.
Yet when change occurs
I reach out in faith by recalling
the words of Saint Teresa of Avila:

"Let nothing disturb you, let nothing frighten you,
everything passes away except God.
God alone is sufficient."

I pray that my faith will grow firmer
no matter how my present situation changes
and for the courage to go on living a good life
despite my imperfections and weaknesses.
Well aware that each day is a step closer

to a spiritual life of love and peace unchanging
with all heavenly certainty.

EXPECTATIONS

Placing expectations on people I've known in the past
has led me on occasion to feel bitter disappointment
whenever those anticipations came crashing down.
Limiting such expectations on anyone has given me
a freer mind to think more defensively and independently
to the point of feeling reassured that dashed confidences
will pain me less in the future.
Yet having given up the trust I once held in others,
I can't help but feel a twinge of disappointment
at not expecting a little more
patience and compassion
of myself.

DREAMS

I believe there have been times when family members
have reached out in spirit for no other reason
but to alleviate a little suffering
by offering gifts of comfort and peace.

During my first year in Alberta,
my Great Aunt Mary Ann,
whom I had known my whole life, died at age 99.
My heavy heart longed to be home to say goodbye
until I had a most uplifting dream.
In it, a much younger version of Mary Ann
stood smiling at me
as she performed a lively step dance.

When I awoke, I felt that she was happy and at peace,
and I never worried about her after that.

When our Nana Alma died, I flew home
and was able to grieve with my family.
Before I departed for Alberta,
I wanted to ask relatives for something of hers
to take back with me,
but I never summoned up the courage.
Months later, I knew the opportunity to ask
had passed, and it was bothering me.
It was then that I dreamt of our grandmother
knitting in her favourite rocking chair.
I watched her as she got up
and walked over to me and said,
"I'm sorry you didn't get what you wanted."
Looking into her eyes, I felt every word,
and all discontentment melted away.
It was so real that I consider that dream
my fondest keepsake from my nana
to this very day.

NOT SO FAR AWAY

———

When thinking of loved ones who have passed on ahead,
though they be out of sight, don't think of them as dead.
Their souls still watch over, much closer than you think
as you work your garden or wash plates in the sink.
You need never fear death or the place where you'll go,
since they'll come to show you the way so you will know.
Heaven's not so distant, just so you are aware,
seeming within arm's reach when those you love are there.

WHOLE AGAIN

I wish I could always choose
the kind and unselfish path,
but I often stumble and fall.
I know deep down that I can be better
at my soul's work
as I believe God intended for me.
The love I feel for my brothers and sisters
is at times a weak spark compared to
the brilliant light of God's love for us.
His is a love so powerful and moving
that when I allow myself in silence
to be touched deeply by it
I am blinded with tears,
humbled by the knowledge that despite
my weaknesses and wrongdoings,
I am still loved.
Soon a joyful composure emerges
with the realization that all my sins
have long since been forgiven.

LEANING ON GOD

When I was ready to settle down I leaned on God.
I knew I needed more love and support in my life
so I wrote an appeal and read it faithfully each night.
Not knowing how long it would take
for my prayer to be answered,
I persevered for several weeks until it happened.
Sitting in a pew at church one Sunday,
a beautiful young woman came and sat down beside me.
She had come with one of the female choir members

and had recently moved from Calgary.
That young woman eventually became my wife.
Looking back, I always knew God was good,
but I never fully realized how He really delivers!
It's not always easy to believe in the power of prayer
because it often takes time before the results are apparent.
Trust in the power of your petition and be persistent.
He will hear your voice.

FOLLOW YOUR HEART

If you are ever thinking of marrying
a woman from the Philippines,
it is important to listen to your heart
and not the judgement of others.
Do not let her slip away
because of what your friends or family might say.
My own mother asked me with dismay,
"What will the children look like?"
My late grandfather inquired,
"What side of the war did they fight on?"
I had to laugh because they only wanted
to see me happy and meant no harm.
If you love her, you've already seen beyond
the physical differences, the imperfect English,
or her current economic status.
You could have a beautiful wife who is not only loyal
and family oriented, but a positive and genuine life partner.
Embrace her now and the home, loving children,
and happy life you've always desired.
When you are truly content, you won't care about
what people might think or say anymore.
Or you can watch her leave,

and years from now when you're older,
you'll have plenty of time to rethink the choices made,
dwelling on the one you let get away,
alone with a heart
full of regret.

IT ALL STARTS AND ENDS WITH GOD

My mother sang my praises, saying how good of me it was
helping my sister-in-law from the Philippines by letting her live with us
while she worked as a caregiver for the family next door.
I basked in the glow of her affirmations until I hung up the phone.
It was then that it dawned on me that she had it all backwards,
since it was I who owed words of praise.

If it weren't for my parents, my wife and I wouldn't have been
in any position to help anyone, since it was only due
to their unselfish sacrifices that we'd built a house with only
a modest mortgage to look after.

I must also acknowledge the tenacity of the Campbell family
for not giving up on the process and for providing
a safe working environment, an income,
and the support required for my sister-in-law
to eventually bring her family over.

And who can forget my sister-in-law's family,
who were apart from each other for three years
working toward the goal of a new life together in Canada.
It's hard to fathom the sacrifices that each
family member endured to make their dream a reality.

All my wife and I did was lend support and pass along
some of the abundant blessings that we have received.
That is why the sincerest of praises should start and end with God,

who makes all things possible, for providing what we have today,
and for bringing our extended family together
from opposite sides of His creation.

WANTS AND NEEDS

Discontentment reigns supreme
when I allow my wants to obscure
the limitless bounty I have around me.
How many times have I heard
that money can't solve our problems,
yet I let my wantonness for it
distract me from what I am truly rich in?
I would be so much happier
if I focused solely on my family
and the priceless blessings they bring.
For it truly makes me
an incredibly wealthy man.

INADEQUACIES

We all feel unworthy and inadequate
from time to time. It finds us all
regardless of gender, ethnicity, or station in life.
At any time, unworthiness is capable
of robbing myself of any present contentment,
simply by reminding me of my inadequacies.
I have learned that there is never enough money,
possessions, education, or acclamations
to permanently alleviate the self-perception
that I am lacking in one way or another.
So instead of taking more from life
I've focused on giving instead.

The practice of giving just the right amount
blesses and connects both the giver and receiver
with a deep sense of contentment, humility, and joy.
It was through giving that I have been
brought the closest to accepting,
appreciating, and loving who I am,
despite my insecurities.

SUMMING IT UP

Oneness is summed up
by the single addition
of unselfish acts.

ANXIETY

The loneliest part of my life
was when I allowed my anxiety
to shy me away from people and opportunities.
The most inauthentic part of my life
was when I drank too much to drown my fears
and, with it, my good judgement.
The best part of my life unfolded
after I understood what anxiety was,
recognized how it affected me,
and accepted the fact
that I was still a good person
despite it.

CRIMES AGAINST CHILDREN

Most people do not want to talk about certain subjects,
and the sexual abuse of children is one of them.
Innocent victims suffer in silence and in secret.
Some keep their painful experiences hidden into adulthood,
while others prefer to carry them to their grave.
Perpetrators of these sexual crimes prefer it this way
so their actions will not be brought to light.
Even after the offenders have moved on,
the adverse effects continue to punish the victim
in the form of depression, body image issues,
self-abusive tendencies, or worse.
Time does not necessarily heal these types of wounds,
but some cope better than others.
So the truth can be known and justice can be served;
some courageously share their experiences, but not all do.
Sometimes the process is just too messy and painful.
Whether a victim comes forward or decides to live with the secrets
is really up to that person to choose.
Whatever road they take, we can all pray, without judgement,
that each finds healing, strength, and peace.
Whether they are ready or willing to forgive,
that too is a choice that is theirs to make.

FORGIVENESS

Forgiveness is when we cure the ill will felt against another.
While resentment is an understandable part of our human nature,
it is to our advantage to remedy it with a prescription
of prayer, humility, and forgiveness.
Jesus taught us from the cross that there was no place in Heaven
for hatred or for holding grudges.

Though Judas betrayed him, Peter denied Him,
Caiaphas condemned Him, the crowds spat on Him,
Pilate washed his hands of Him,
and the Roman soldiers crucified Him,
Jesus forgave them all.
Sooner or later, so must I.

FORGETFULNESS

My mother's memory is not what it used to be,
but that is okay. Her cheerful and gentle nature
still shines through each time I speak with her.
Though many think of forgetfulness as a flaw,
it could very well be one of the greatest gifts from God.
Just think about how much happier people would be
if they only forgot moments when they weren't at their best.
Imagine if we could simply delete our fears and regrets,
or erase all grudges, resentments, and judgements
we hold against each other. Would it free us to live a better life?
Heaven might be a lot like that, but down here,
I'm afraid I still have work to do,
learning and growing from all my mistakes,
while ignoring or resisting
every temptation to repeat them.

TEMPTATION

When temptation enters my day,
I choose to keep it at bay.
I shut it down and look away.

TURN, TURN, TURN

We all like to feel that we're good at something,
and for me it has been storytelling and teaching.
Practising my craft for as long as I have,
I would sometimes get to thinking
that I was getting pretty good at it.
There may have been times when I even considered
myself as one of the best grade 5 teachers ever!
But as the sun begins to set on my career,
I find my feelings of indispensability
being eclipsed by undeniable sadness.
Not for the future students who will be taught
by new and innovative teachers,
but sad in knowing that one day
I will be replaced, and the world will continue
to invariably turn.

MAY TOLERANCE AND FORGIVENESS GROW

I remember them as clear as day,
the raw emotions on each young face.
Students of mine only ten years old,
upset about something they'd been told.
Walking from town during lunch that day,
two teens passed going the other way.
They didn't recognize who they were
yet were greeted with a racial slur.
The boys could hardly believe their ears
when "Dirty Indians" rang out clear.
They came to class hurting and confused,
telling me about what they went through.
I could write down what I said, maybe,

but emotion got the best of me.
If I could have that moment redone,
I'd try to address them as my sons.
I am so sorry, boys, you were hurt
by those nameless ones out flinging dirt.
You did nothing wrong along the way
to deserve the words heard today.
You put others first and are so kind;
two nicer fellows I could not find.
But there are people who just don't care
about right or wrong or what is fair.
They're full of anger and disrespect,
not kind or friendly as you'd expect.
They verbalize sharp and harmful things,
not concerned with how much pain they'll bring.
They think they're right and that it's okay
to injure those who don't look the same.
But it's wrong to malign each other,
who under the skin are our brothers.
So don't believe the words that were said;
they don't know you, so their words are dead.
Do not let ignorance cloud your mind;
recognize God's truth and don't be blind.
God loves all and has favourites none;
in Heaven or earth we should be one.
We are called to serve by the Lord above,
to love one another as we are loved.
They were wrong when they put you down,
but don't let angry thoughts stick around.
Don't follow down those paths so mean,
and you'll walk away with conscience clean.
Show tolerance wherever you go;
be yourself and let forgiveness grow.

GOD HAS NO FAVORITES

It is our comparative nature
that has the potential to divide us.
From an early age, children can differentiate
between people, but they can be very accepting.
When our youth are taught to believe
that some people are superior or inferior to others,
a child's perception rapidly narrows.
Bigotry begins as a harmful seed that is implanted
into the fertile minds of the young.
The fruit is an adult mind
that judges people as being greater or less than themselves
based solely on what they observe.
It's easy to distinguish differences, but it takes wisdom
to recognize our similarities on a deeper level.
When we teach our children to love themselves,
to understand our commonalities with others
while accepting and appreciating our differences,
the process of respecting others begins.
These are the seeds that we need to be planting
so that the next crop of sons and daughters
will be well rooted in the truth
of our connectedness and equally
under one God.

JOURNEYING WITH THE STORYTELLER

This storytelling section is my favourite
because of the people included in it.
Most were older family members who were willing
to share some of their life experiences.
Before my teaching journey began,
I was fortunate to have the opportunities
to sit down with them as they recounted
their stories to me on a mini tape recorder.
Their compassionate and gentle natures
shone through their words like the sunlight
filtering through the summer leaves.
It's this kind of warmth that I wish
to pass down to our own children.
My papa, nana, and two great aunts have since passed,
yet they still speak to us from these pages.
It is an honour to bring them to life again, in a sense,
and to have them accompany us
on this storytelling journey.

THE TELLING OF A STORY

Who doesn't love to hear a good story?
How many of us have actually had the chance?
It's rare to hear a good storyteller today,
but if you happen upon one, take the time to listen.
Put your life on hold and stay awhile.
Experience a simpler form of connection
that harkens back to your earliest ancestors
before the necessities of reading, writing,
or today's technological distractions.
Clear your mind and be fully present
with all of your senses sitting at the ready.
Prepare to be awed just by focusing

on the teller's facial expressions and actions
as you let the words guide you forward
like a flashlight in a darkened mysterious world.
Let the emotion move you, the pauses suspend you,
the humour lighten you, and the terror
tingle you to the bone as you walk back home
or try to snuggle into bed after dark
as the wind outside your window
whistles and whispers your name.

THE TALL MAN

AS TOLD BY DONALD (JOHNNY MURDOCK) MAC DONALD

I was only very young then, maybe eight or nine. We had a horse, wagon, and a few cows. Of course, there was only my mother (and my brothers). My father had died years before. One morning we went out to the barn, and a couple of times, we noticed that the horse would be sweating, but we didn't know why. But this morning my mother went out to the barn, and the horse was all covered with froth. And you could see the marks of the harness straps on him, because the sweat had hardened up in froth. God, we didn't know what in the heck had happened to the horse.

We never found out, but many years later after the war was over a cousin of mine asked me, "Did you ever find out what happened to the horse?"

"No, we never did."

"Do you want to know?"

"Yeah, it would be nice to know."

"I was one of them," my cousin said. (Laughter) "We put the harness on the horse in the barn and then took the horse out. We went by the house and down the road till we got behind the barn. Somebody else went up and took the wagon down so that the horse and wagon wouldn't make any sound."

"What were you doing?" I asked.

"We were going to steal apples. We were stealing the apples over at Hawley's Hill, the other side of Mabou."

There was a great big orchard down below the road there at that time. So they went to the orchard and tied the horse. I think there were four of them, in their teens. Some were up the tree and some were on the ground picking the apples.

They saw this man coming in from the road, a great big tall fellow. Never saw a man as tall in all their lives, and he was walking slowly toward them. They jumped down off the tree, forgot about the apples, and took off for the wagon. Jumped on the wagon, out on the road they went, put the whip on the horse. And this fellah turned after them. The road was very crooked then. You could only go up a little ways and then you'd be out of sight. The guy was walking, and they were on the gallop, a hard gallop with the horse. And every turn they went around, that man was still behind them, walking. It scared the life out of them. They went all the way down until they got on a straight stretch down the Brook Village Road. The guy was still walking behind them, and the horse was going. They didn't know what it was. If you could walk behind a horse that was galloping, I don't know what you'd be. So they galloped all the way home and almost killed the horse. That's why the horse was covered in froth the next morning. We didn't know until then. That was years later after the war. I guess he got brave to tell the story. (Laughter) That was the end of stealing apples for them.

WEST YORKSHIRE RIDING COMPANY IN 1941
AS TOLD BY ALMA (HODGES) MAC DONALD

The company was looking for bus conductresses because all the boys were in the army. You'd come into the bus station and there would be a queue a mile long, and they'd be cursing you because they couldn't get on the bus; you were only allowed sixty-four people on: fifty-two seated and twelve standing. They'd be trying to crowd on the bus, and you'd be trying to push them off. They always called me the "Little Irish Lassie." Blue eyes and quick tempered! (Laughter) There was never nonsense; we wouldn't put up with anything from them, because if you did, they'd pick at you. Then a lot would try to get away without paying, you know. You had two decks to look after. The buses never stopped, running seven days a week. Everything would start at five in the morning; sometimes we wouldn't be finished until twelve at night, and you'd have to be up again next morning. Sometimes you didn't get a break; you'd be running late, and you wouldn't get your dinner. You'd have to keep going.

In Bradford, we were a little too close. They were dropping bombs all around, so we just stopped the bus, and everybody got out. All of a sudden, we heard this screaming from one of the houses nearby, and the driver went running. Here it was a woman in the house; she was standing on a chair, and there was a little mouse. They were dropping bombs all around (and) she was more scared of the mouse. (Laughter)

IN THE NAME OF GOD, WHAT DO YOU WANT?
AS TOLD BY MARY ANN (MAC LELLAN) MAC EACHERN

That story about the women milking the cows, you heard that one, did you? When my father was at the old place, there were two (women) up there. The women had two cows and a churn, and they would make butter. One day they had no salt to salt the butter, so one of them went over to a neighbour's house to get a bowl of salt. That was okay; she got it and she made the butter. After that, the woman who borrowed the salt died, and she never returned the salt home.

Here weren't the neighbours, some women out milking the cows in the pen, and they saw this woman coming. It was the one who didn't send the salt home. They recognized the woman as the one who died. They got scared. They didn't wait to milk the cows (and) they took off home. They told the priest about seeing the woman. The priest told them that if they see her again, ask her what she wants "in the name of God."

The next day the same women were in milking the cows, and the ghost came again. One of them asked her, "What in the name of God do you want? I'm scared."

The (ghost) woman said, "I forgot to send that salt home. Will you please send it home, and you won't see me anymore."

So they got the salt (from the other old woman) and then sent it home. They never saw her anymore.

BETSY THE HELPFUL GHOST
DETAILS PROVIDED BY BESSIE (HODGES) LONGLEY

My great-great-great grandma,
Betsy (Bell) Claxton,
always seemed to be there
when her family needed her most.
She appeared to Great-Grandpa Neuber
when his wife, Sarah, went into labour
and sent him home running and shaking
from the Kicking Horse Pub.
She came through the window and informed
my great uncle's son that his wife, Enid,
had been in an accident and would get better.
She walked into Great Aunt Bessie's room
and told her not to worry about her baby,
who had been born premature and died,
saying she would look after her.
Betsy always seemed to be there to help
whenever there was trouble in her family.
Though I must confess, if I ever
caught a glimpse of a little old woman
wearing a black skirt and dark grey blouse
tight at the neck, with ghostly grey hair
floating in my direction to the rescue,
I believe that I'd be a lot less relieved
than I would be utterly terrified.

60

THE HUNT
AS RETOLD BY MY FATHER, WILLIE MAC LELLAN

The police were down checking every night,
so the fellas couldn't get out to do any jacking.
The neighbour had a big bull in the barn,
and the guys tied a spotlight between his horns.
When it was dark, they let the bull out into the field.
The bull was walking around
with his head bobbing up, down, and around
with the light on.
The police saw this, so they crossed the fence
and ran up the field, right up beside the bull.
"Stop in the name of the law!"
They just made the fence back and no more.

MY STAY IN BOURNEMOUTH, ENGLAND * 1943
AS TOLD BY DONALD (JOHNNY MURDOCK) MAC DONALD

I went down to Bournemouth, but there wasn't a soul there. As a rule, Bournemouth was the place where the soldiers all went to be dispersed. After fifteen days in the hospital, I landed in between batches, and I was the only one around. They told me about a house up there on the hill. There were great big summer homes that were evacuated for troops with nobody in them.

"Here's a blanket. Find a bed and go to sleep there tonight."

I was so tired, it didn't matter where I slept, as long as they put me somewhere. That night, I went to bed and slept like a log.

I came down in the morning to get breakfast, and someone said, "Were you scared last night?"

"No. Why?" I asked.

"There's an ack-ack gun behind that house and it was going all night."
(Laughter) The sound from that gun would wake the dead. I never heard
a thing.

THE UNSINKABLE HANNAH DOBSON
DETAILS PROVIDED BY BESSIE (HODGES) LONGLEY

Great-Great-Grandmother Hannah (Claxton)
married an American, William Dobson, in 1895 in England.
His parents overseas did not approve of their union for unknown reasons.
Perhaps they had better prospects in mind for their handsome son,
more suitable than Hannah, who already had a daughter out of wedlock.
Nevertheless, they came over to visit him and his family in England.
When they were ready to return to the United States,
William offered to see them off at the train station,
where his parents would travel on to the port of departure.
William never returned.
Hannah rushed to make inquiries at the Crook Station
and learned that her husband had bought a ticket
and boarded the train with his parents.
From there she hurried to the Liverpool docks
to find that his ship had sailed.
Hannah wouldn't let them get the better of her.
She found out when the next ship departure was
and hastened home to pack a trunk.
She left her daughter, Sarah Elizabeth, with her mother, Betsy,
and headed back to Liverpool to buy a ticket aboard the SS *Rhynland*,
which set sail for America on June 4, 1902.
As luck would have it, the *Rhynland* turned out to be a faster ship
than her husband's, and she reached Philadelphia first.
When William and his parents disembarked from the vessel
they were shocked to find my great-great-grandmother, Hannah,
standing there waiting for them.

From that point, and throughout the waves of time,
Hannah and William were inseparable.

THE WOMAN IN BLACK
AS TOLD BY DONALD (JOHNNY MURDOCK) MAC DONALD
———

My brother Jim Willie Mac Donald was born in 1921 and was the youngest of the boys. He had a strange experience while he was still living at the old place. An apparition in a black dress appeared at the foot of his bed after he had turned in for the night. Jim couldn't see her face, and he got scared. He would not speak to her; he pulled the blankets over his head and when he looked again, she was gone.

Jim moved away to cut pulp in Maine and then moved to Toronto to work for the city. It was in either Maine or Toronto that the apparition in the black dress appeared for a second time at the foot of his bed. He would not speak to her, and he pulled the covers over his head again. After this second sighting, he went to see a priest about what he had seen. The priest told Jim Willie to have a Mass said for the woman, even though he did not know who she was. The Mass was said, and he never saw the woman again.

63 |

UNWELCOME MESSENGER
AS TOLD BY MARY ANN (MAC LELLAN) MAC EACHERN
———

It's called the *Taibhse* in Gaelic. The bird is (a messenger) from the other world. When you see "the bird," it's a sign that someone is going to die.

My mother and father were milking the cows in the pen, and this bird sat on the fence and started screeching. The bird followed them clear into the milk house, and when it got in, it made another screech. The next morning, someone came to tell us that (my brother) Allan was killed at Marble Mountain (quarry.) A rock hit him here (on the forehead) and killed him.

My husband, Charlie, saw the bird too. Charlie went down to get water at the well, and a bird made a screech. Charlie paid no attention to it. He got the water and then the bird followed him back up (to the house) and made another screech. When he came in, he saw it try to fly into the house through the window. The Monday after that, Charlie was in the woods, and Jim and Alexander had gone after the mare in Glencoe. A knock came at the door, and the priest was there.

"Oh Mary," he said, "I have sad news for you. Jim was killed today."

(Tears) I couldn't stop crying. He had a scissor bit and he put that in the mare. He twisted it and it cut the mare and, of course, she had to kick. Poor Jim didn't have the rope long enough. She got him here somewhere (on the forehead.)

We were over (at the Mac Millans') for a frolic; they were hauling pulp. Jessie was at home with me, and we were making biscuits. Alec Dan (Mac Millan) came home late.

"Wait and I'll drive you home," he said.

As soon as we got on the sleigh, a bird came, and an awful screech rang through my head. The horses got scared. "What's that? I said.

He said, "That's the big bird."

We drove a little, and the bird followed us back and forth. It scared the wits out of me. Eeeeeeeach!!! It sounded something like that. His father, Neil, died a few days after that.

LOVE IS PATIENT

DETAILS PROVIDED BY BESSIE (HODGES) LONGLEY

After buying an old house, my great uncle and aunt, Ronnie and Bessie Longley, lived on the second storey and opened a small store on the ground floor. For the first three years they never experienced anything of the paranormal nature.

One evening before closing, an elderly woman walked in and strolled around the shop as if she had no interest in buying. When she stopped to look up their stairs, Bessie went over and asked if she needed anything.

The woman smiled and said that she just wanted to see the old place again. She introduced herself as Joyce Burton, a retired school teacher, and explained that she had visited here on many occasions years ago. Being close to closing time for the store, Bessie offered the older lady tea, and she accepted. As Ronnie locked up for the night, Joyce and Bessie got down to the business of tea and conversation. Joyce shared her story of how she was to marry the young man who once lived there with his family.

"We were to be married after the (Great) War. He joined the merchant navy, but his ship was torpedoed." Sombrely she added, "I never courted after that."

After tea, Joyce took Bessie on a tour through her own home, unlocking many of the secrets each room held.

"There used to be a piano in this room," she told Bessie. "He used to play, and we would sing together."

Joyce told Bessie that after her beau died, she continued to visit his mother and father, and after each of her visitations, his parents would hear footsteps or the piano play after they had gone to bed. Although they were the only ones in the house, they weren't afraid because they assumed it was the ghost of their son. Bessie informed her that she had never noticed anything out of the ordinary since they'd moved in. Joyce finished her tea, and Bessie invited her new friend back for another visit to the house. She accepted.

After she had gone, Bessie went through her nightly ritual of closing all of the fire doors that separated the rooms. The next morning, Ronnie was up first and not long after informed Bessie that she had forgotten to close the fire doors the night before. Bessie protested, saying that she had, yet they were open. For the next few nights, the doors remained shut as usual, until Joyce came over for another evening of tea and conversation. After the visit, she walked home and Bessie shut all the fire doors before turning in. By next morning, the interior doors were open wide. This pattern of the doors mysteriously opening after a visit from her friend Joyce reoccurred time after time.

Eventually, Bessie's friend took a bad turn with cancer. The evening Joyce Burton died, she asked Bessie if she would be able to "lay her out" for her funeral, which meant doing her hair, makeup, and getting her washed and dressed. At her friend's bedside, Bessie agreed and said goodbye.

When Bessie arrived back at the store, Ronnie was still up. It was around 10:00 p.m. when all of a sudden all five fire doors slammed shut, one after another. Bessie said to Ronnie, "She's gone," and Ronnie said to Bessie, "And he's gone with her." All stayed quiet from that point on.

THE BLANKET

COLLECTED IN RESERVE MINES, CAPE BRETON,
AND RETOLD BY LEN MAC LELLAN

Our mother walked up our gravel lane and into our front yard.
Through the kitchen window, my sisters and I eyed her
as she stopped in front of her vegetable garden.
We knew who it was because she was wearing the same dress
we last saw her in. Too scared to move, we watched her
out the window for a few moments, and then she was gone.
When Dad came home from working in the pit,
we all rushed out and told him that we'd seen Mom.
When he saw that we were serious, he calmed us down
and said not to worry. This was her way of saying goodbye.
But the next day, she was back again waiting at the garden.
Dad wasn't home, so my oldest sister said
that she was going out to speak to her.
We stared from the window as she walked up to our mother
and asked what she wanted, in the name of God.
Mom spoke to her. My sister was soon walking back to the house,
and Mom was gone again.
We met our sister at the door and followed her upstairs,
where she found the blanket that our mother
had borrowed in the winter.
Together we returned it to our neighbour, as Mom had wanted.

With her conscience cleared, she could finally rest
and we never saw our mother's ghost after that.

RUNNING THE FARM
AS RETOLD BY MY FATHER, WILLIE MAC LELLAN

Do you know the story about the big farm down here?
A gentleman from the Agricultural Department came
(and) he wanted to inspect around the farm.
The farmer didn't want him nosing around.
"Well, I've got a card in my pocket here that says that
I can go anywhere I want to on your farm
and you can't do a thing about it."
"Okay," the farmer said, and the Agricultural guy
took off down through the field.
After a while, the farmer heard awful hollering and screaming.
He went over to the fence and looked down the field.
The Agricultural fellow was running as hard as he could go,
arms waving and hollering, and a big bull right behind him.
So the farmer hollered to him,
"Show him your card! Show him your card!" (Laughter)

WE REMEMBER THEM

I wish I had more stories to pass on from relatives who had served in the World Wars, though I understand why I don't.

My grandfather, Alec Dan Mac Lellan, was drafted in 1917, yet never told his family before he was shipped out overseas. According to his military records, he served in the front lines in France with the 25th Battalion and was wounded by shrapnel. Little was said to his family about his war experiences or the time spent after the war exhuming the dead for reinternment in Commonwealth grave sites. When asked by his youngest son years later what the war was like, he was told not to ask such stupid questions. Such stories, it seems, were better left unearthed.

My great-grandfather, Neuber Hodges, also served in the Great War and was wounded by a sniper. The only time he talked about the war was after the second one started. He told his son Phillip that if he was given a long overcoat, he should cut it short because it would only get caught in the barbed wire and he'd never get out. Neuber said he'd seen too many men shot down because they were caught on the wire and couldn't get off.

My great uncle Phillip Hodges served in WW2 and was burned badly after he lit a kerosene blow torch that had been filled with petrol by the enemy. He ran in terror and agony before being tackled and put out. His legs got the worst of it, and he spent months in hospital. He always kept his shirts buttoned to the top to hide his scars.

My great uncle, Murdock Mac Donald, never had a chance to tell stories. He volunteered to join the Royal Canadian Engineers and was killed in Noordeind, Holland on October 21, 1944. According to the Regimental War Diary, they were attempting to dismantle and open a booby-trapped gate near a railway crossing when it exploded. He and two others died together.

Most of the war stories I remember growing up with were shared by my grandfather, Donald (Johnny Murdock) Mac Donald, who volunteered for the Royal Canadian Air Force. He and several other Canadians helped to man a decoy airfield in England. It was around that time that he met his wife, Alma Hodges, at a local dance. They married in England in 1944.

Not all soldiers spoke about the war, unless the listener had been there themselves. Many were not willing to describe the horror of what they had to do or what they had seen done. Maybe it was their way of sparing the innocent the terrible truth of what one person is capable of doing to another human being in battle. I can only respect their silence as I stare at each of their young faces frozen in time behind the framed glass. For the untold service, sacrifices, and suffering many veterans wished to forget, we will forever remember them.

REMEMBRANCE DAY

It's Remembrance Day, and I'm thinking of my grandfather, Alec Dan Mac Lellan. A front line veteran of the Great War, he died in 1968, before I was born. There are a few stories from that time in his life that were retold by his late sister, Mary Ann. However, two experiences he did reveal have survived to this day. The stories concerned two men he knew during that time and the emotional impact they had on him.

The first man was a Mac Eachern from Glendale, Cape Breton, who embarked with Alec Dan on the troopship *Metagama*, which sailed from Halifax on April 7, 1918. We never knew his first name. Glendale is a small place, just down the road from where my grandfather grew up, so they likely knew of each other before the war. Mary Ann knew the fellow my grandfather spoke of, saying that Mr. Mac Eachern "was a nice violin player too." Maybe he too was drafted during that last year of the war and the pair might have a few choice words in Gaelic about that on the way over, but no one can be certain. What we know for sure was what Mary Ann recalled hearing. She said that halfway across the Atlantic Ocean, Mr. Mac Eachern died of a broken heart. In the end, he had no casket as they slipped him over the side of the ship. His final resting place was a watery grave somewhere between the hills of his beloved Glendale home and the dreaded trenches in France.

The second fellow Alec Dan spoke about to his sister was a young soldier from Margaree, Cape Breton, Nova Scotia. Though his name is unknown, Alec Dan said he was only a teenager who might have even lied about his age to get into the service. Alec Dan was thirty-four years old at the time and took the tall lad under his wing. In the trenches, the Margareer was told time and time again to keep his head down by my grandfather. But he didn't always take heed and was killed when he was shot in the head by a sniper. My grandfather told his sister that he cried and prayed for his young friend all night with his rosary beads in hand.

Though we don't know these soldiers by name, or even if they hailed from Glendale or Margaree for certain, they will not be forgotten on this day. For they were once like us, with dreams, a home, and family of their own. A former life to which there would be no return. For these two Cape Bretoners lost so long ago, let these lines be a small remembrance of them.

POST TIME

Memories of PEI from when I was just a boy
revolve around Old Home Week and times of family joy.
But there's one special moment, though I certainly have doubts
if you'll believe this poem when you hear what it's about.
My father Willie used to love those harness racing days,
when he knew scorecards inside out so betting went his way.
Sent my mother, Gloria, to buy a six dollar box
on the three fastest horses, thinking that he had it locked.
But when she sat beside him with the promising ticket,
the numbers she had chosen were mixed up something wicked.
Surely the poorest horses stared up from the blackened print,
not favoured to win, place, or show in a mile or a sprint.
With the race soon beginning and no time for another,
Dad could only shake his head at my innocent mother.
The start gate pulled away and his favourites sped ahead,
leaving the remainder of the field destined to be led.
Whoa, when all of a sudden came an unexpected crash,
leaving the trailing trotters alone for the homeward dash.
Only three lucky pacers were remaining in the chase,
and the ones on Dad's ticket amazingly won the race.
Three hundred fifty dollars was the miraculous prize,
leaving my parents laughing in a sea of mournful sighs.
Really, what were the chances? Impossible to predict
a trio of long shots would be the winners Mom had picked.
My father soon stopped pouting and finally changed his tune,
with smiling so darn easy watching a bust turn to boom.

The moral of the story, whether past or present tense,
trusting your spouse's better judgement makes perfect horse sense.

THE RIGHT DIRECTION

Anxiety overshadowed my final weeks of university, not knowing exactly where my degree would lead me. Walking toward the university cafeteria I saw Mike, a friend I knew through classes. We stopped to say hello and he inquired about my future plans. I honestly told him that my pathway into the future was uncertain, and Mike suggested applying to the University of Maine, where teacher training would begin in the fall.

"You should apply," he encouraged with the utmost enthusiasm.

I told him that I liked the idea of following my mother's footsteps into teaching, but I was doubtful of acceptance because of my mediocre grades. He urged me to apply anyway and sweetened the idea by mentioning that a female friend needed a roommate, so I wouldn't have to worry about a place to live. It was like I was standing on a welcome mat as a door into a career I thought to be inaccessible opened up for me.

In quick succession, I took the steps to apply and was accepted. Soon a student loan was arranged, I met my new roommate, and we moved our belongings into a shared apartment in Claire, New Brunswick, mere walking distance across the border from the University at Fort Kent. Throughout that year and a half, many like-minded companions kindly helped me along on my educational journey, and we each walked away with a teaching degree. All except for Mike, who had a sincere change of heart and returned to Nova Scotia not long after arriving.

I never saw my friend after that, but I thank God for putting him on my path that day. I'd like to shake his hand for delivering the sound advice that steered me in the right direction, to the place where I stand so reflectively today, after twenty-five years of teaching.

SNOWSTORM

I remember it being the most frightening snowstorm I had ever driven through by myself. Not wanting to miss my student teaching classes the next day, I left Sunday afternoon from my home in western Cape Breton and headed east across the island. Little did I know that the next few hours would be a tense slow crawl through a vast curtain of snow. I kept a tight grip on the wheel as I focused on keeping my tires on the two narrow tracks in the deep, slushy snow ahead. Too afraid to stop, turn around, or change the fiddle cassette, I had no choice but to drive on and pray. As darkness descended, the weather began to clear, and I figured that I only had another half hour of driving remaining.

In the distance, I saw headlights approaching down a hill and then suddenly veer across my lane and disappear from sight. My heart dropped, knowing it was unlikely that someone would turn into a driveway at that speed. I slowed as I reached the spot, and saw vehicle tracks leading down a steep embankment. I pulled over and got out. The highway seemed deserted in both directions, and I prayed for the accident not to be too serious or bloody. Not being able to keep my feet, I sat down and began sliding to the bottom of the hill as a boy of about nine or ten passed me running up the slope. He must have been in shock because he never saw me, screaming "Help, help!" as he went.

When I got to the bottom, I found the car banked at a forty-five degree angle. The driver was attempting to calm his five year old daughter, who was crying hysterically. I told the father who I was and asked the little girl her name and what grade she was in. It seemed to calm her down enough to give the dad a chance to shut off the car and gather some belongings. No one was injured, so we helped each other up the slippery embankment and found the man's son still waiting to wave down traffic. The dad wanted a drive home, so I dropped them off not far down the road. They waved thankfully as I drove away.

Thinking back, they might have thought I was a guardian angel or something to that degree, after I appeared out of a snowstorm in my white

Pontiac to bring them home. Who knows? All I know for certain was how thankful to God I was for getting me safely across the island that day and for allowing me to help a family in need.

HEADING TO ALBERTA

In August of 1996, I left Judique, Cape Breton, Nova Scotia to begin my teaching career in the west. Along for the drive was a fellow from Newfoundland who was also heading out for a job in Alberta. On the spiritual side of things, I prayed for St. Joseph to accompany us on our 5,600-kilometre journey, figuring if he got Mary to Bethlehem, he might be willing to guide along two stray sheep from the east.

All was well until the second day when the alternator died in Deep River, Ontario. But lucky for us, we were just down the road from a Canadian Tire Service Centre. With only enough money for food and fuel along the route, I called my mother in Cape Breton, and she agreed to pay for a rebuilt alternator at the Canadian Tire back home, and they would wire the money ahead. Before my mom hung up, she suggested that I visit my great uncle, Allan Mac Donald, who resided in Deep River with his family. Of all the places to break down, I was amazed to hear of family nearby. I asked the serviceman if he knew an Allan Mac Donald, and he smiled, saying that he'd known him all his life. He happily pointed out the directions to Allan's home and told us to be back in an hour and a half. Allan and his wife showed us much kindness before they sent us on our way with full bellies and gifts tucked under my arm.

Before long, we were back on the road feeling refreshed and thankful. Two hours later, we found ourselves driving through a North Bay downpour. At a red light, pungent smoke oozed into the car, and the Newfoundlander cried out that we were on fire. Not knowing what to do, I pulled onto the traffic median in the middle of the divided street and stopped. We quickly stepped out into the pouring rain but were unable to unlatch the hood because of the flames reaching out from beneath it. My buddy and I grabbed a bag each, thinking the vehicle was going up in a

73|

blaze of glory. No one stopped to help us in the rainstorm, so I walked out in front of a van to ask for assistance. The driver assured me he would call for help, and I thanked him.

My buddy and I made our way down the street with our spirits hanging lower than our soggy suitcases. The workers at a KFC let us leave our luggage behind as we turned back toward the fire trucks and flashing lights. The car hood was up, and the fire was out, thankfully, by the time we walked back, but much of the front end was either burned or melted on the ground. *What now?* I thought. *Now we're stuck in the middle of Canada with no running car and only basic collision car insurance.*

In desperation, all I could do was pray. It was then that I overheard the firemen conversing as they stared into the engine compartment. To one of them, it appeared as though the fire had started with the alternator. I piped up and informed them that I just had a rebuilt alternator installed at the Canadian Tire in Deep River. One of the firemen added that the second largest Canadian Tire store in Canada was just a few blocks away, and that he would call to tell them what had happened.

Soon, a tow truck was on scene to haul our smoldering vehicle to the store, and after telling our story to the store manager, we were driven to a motel and asked to wait. After a consultation with the insurance adjustor, the store owner called and said that the front end of the car was going to be rebuilt free of charge! We could hardly believe it. Utilizing new and used parts, the service centre technicians worked throughout the night, and by morning, we happily drove away with a better running automobile than we had leaving Nova Scotia.

A couple of days later, after dropping my travelling mate off near Edmonton, I arrived in Valleyview, Alberta, just days before classes started. To this day I am so thankful to St. Joseph for guiding us out west safely, and that the fire didn't start in the middle of nowhere. I'll always feel a debt of gratitude to Canadian Tire, and the neighbourly people in North Bay, who kindly went out of their way to help two stranded sheep reach their new western flocks.

PRAYER SWEAT

From among the poplar embers,
the grandfather cobbles were plucked
and into Mother Earth all placed
within our domed gathering space
beneath the sweat lodge ceiling tucked
many moons back in November.

With the human circle now one,
darkness fell as the door flap dropped
and the dripping spruce bow taken
from the brimming pail was shaken
upon those sizzling sacred rocks,
sending steam scorching like the sun.

Such discomfort I've never known,
as if seared from my face to waist
while the prayers in Cree had begun,
and from behind my towel that hung
I too spoke litanies with haste
in a most intense fervent tone.

After the third prayer round was said,
we crawled out on our hands and feet
into the winter day's embrace,
and onto thankful hands were placed
salmon, berries, and corn to eat
while resting upon cool snow beds.

And soon we returned to the flow
of sweat and words swiftly chanted
until the last round of prayers ceased
and my distress succumbed to peace

as I believed requests granted
and true blessings had been bestowed.

On that initiation day,
my baptism of sweat and fire
dually prepared me for trials
I would confront once in a while
at the school for which I was hired,
and everything would be okay.

And so it was over the years
no matter how I was tested
on these western trails travelled,
my career never unravelled,
since my faith was firmly rested
upon He who had led me here.

DEAR CAPE BRETON

———

Land of my home, land that I love, fare thee well.
I have left you once more but have since longed to be with you.
My ears strain to hear your babbling brooks and crashing waves
that once climbed your rocky shore to greet me.
I long to listen to the soft summer breeze as it whispers
through your trees, and the air so full of the rich music
and kind conversation of your inhabitants.
Though I am here, my thoughts are with the people
and place I care for most. Through my mind's eye,
I see your spruce-clad hills sloping down to your rugged coastline,
a scene that still lifts my spirit above your highest misty highlands.
You still stir feelings that go far beyond any words
meant to express them.

LEN MAC LELLAN

In your past you've been the proudest of foster parents,
taking in those who were disowned or driven away
from old Mother Scotland. You welcomed them
and offered them a new life, supported by your land and sea.
To their descendants, you extended the same abundance,
but many wanted more than what they saw before them.
Time after time you have lamented the leaving
of generations of grandsons and granddaughters
who had grown too large for you and could not stay.
You were helpless to stop them, for they heard
the promises of a better life far and away.

Sadly, I have followed in their footsteps, drawn away
like the many before me. I am going because I feel I must go,
aware of the much greater thing I am leaving behind: my heart.
It remains there among a people of the warmest kindness
and greatest sincerity on earth, from whom
a friendly word and deed is easily found.
For you are enveloped in a spirit and kinship
that runs deeper than your coal seams and Lakes of Bras d'Or
and extends wider than the ocean that surrounds you.
Though the cold winds will continue to swirl around
your hills and glens, one may still feel your warmth
of hospitality and home.

I have often dreamt of becoming a part of you again,
like the many who do return, having never forgotten
the beauty of what they had left behind.
Until then, your rivers and streams will continue to swell
from the tears of those who must leave you.
For you are like no other island, a moon among stars,
and for you I harbour a love like no other
that began when I was born
and will endure long after I am gone.

BONNIE PRINCE

Bonnie Prince Charlie, it may have been better
if you had never gone over to Scotland,
but in the long run, I'm glad that you did.
Our ancestors fought for you in 1746 and lost,
but poverty, hunger, and intolerance
continued to be the most persistent foes.
As the population grew, rented land
and subsistence farming were not enough,
and sheep promised more to the land owners
than the poor masses.
Whether they left the highlands and islands on their own
or were sent away, they crossed the vast western ocean
to new lands with their Gaelic, traditions,
Catholic faith, a hardiness to survive, and each other.
That first generation over here endured
unimaginable suffering and hardship
as they literally cleared the way
for successive waves of descendants born.
These would inherit what their ancestors never had:
land of their own, freedom, an education,
better opportunities to earn a living,
and a new language.
The common man or woman lives and prospers
better today in Canada than King George II
ever did back in the Old Country.
Though some still may lament the loss
of so many through emigration,
the reality was that they could not stay.
So Bonnie Prince, though it may have been better
had you not gone over, I'd like to extend

a wholehearted *Tapadh leat,*
that you did.

OUT OF MY HANDS

I remember how awfully scary my friend's car was to drive. Each time I took my foot off the gas pedal, it would begin to accelerate like it had a will of its own. The only time it didn't accelerate was on the upslope. I recall having to drive into a snowbank just to slow the car down enough to use the brakes. Once it was in park, the engine would rev up high, as if the car was going to rear up on its hind wheels. The vehicle even took a few moments to sputter to a stop after the key was removed from the ignition.

After paying for two hours of diagnostic work in Edmonton, Alberta, a mechanic couldn't find a cause for the problem, leaving us an uneasy sense of relief as we readied for the four-hour winter trek up north. Before we departed, we prayed to get home safely.

On the highway, the car felt like a wild stallion bolting across smooth open pastures. Just before Fox Creek, the situation became dire when we noticed that both lanes of the undivided highway were now grey with ice. We knew nothing was open, since it was a holiday, but we needed to pull off before our untrustworthy steed crossed the centre line or charged for the woods to our right. As before, the brakes slowed us down just enough that I could unsteadily manoeuvre the car onto a utility road and into a parking lot. With my foot to the floor, it slowed to a rolling stop, and I slammed it into park. The engine roared to life before dying a slow death with the turn of the key. We were so relieved, but now what? Businesses were closed and we saw no one around. My anxiety grew at the thought of taming this wild beast of a car the rest of the way home.

All of a sudden, out of nowhere, a truck pulled up beside us. We looked over as the stranger rolled down his window.

"Are you having a problem with your car?" the fellow asked.

In unison we blurted, "Yes!"

"Can I take a look?"

He didn't have to ask twice as we popped the hood and told him about the car's troubling symptoms. With a puny flashlight in hand, within three minutes he had pulled a thin piece of white plastic from somewhere, and he told us it was holding something open and the car was getting too much gas. We couldn't believe it. After a huge thank you from us, he drove off into the night like an unsung western hero.

From that point on, the car worked perfectly. Many times since I've thanked God for placing that cowboy on our path and for helping us safely reach our northern pastures.

TEARS OF JOY

A tear ran down my daughter's cheek as her eyes
looked up at me through brown shimmering pools.
Mere minutes before, she was more than happy
to spend the cash she was given on Christmas presents
for her sister and brother. On our way to the store exit,
we heard a bell and saw the Salvation Army kettle.
I told her they collected money to help people
through tough times and whispered to her a kind suggestion.
She walked up to the kettle and slowly emptied her purse
of all the change she thought was hers for the keeping.
As she walked back to me, her tears weren't hard to notice,
so I gave my daughter a hug and told her I was so proud
that she had given so much and that Jesus would be proud too.
As we drove away from the store, half crying in the back seat
I heard Alexis say, "I feel so happy."
Happy perhaps after discovering what joy can be gained
when one empties themselves for the sake of others.

THE UNICORN

Anna was so proud of her miniature glass unicorn, as if it were sculpted to be cradled in her five-year-old palm. A gift intricately detailed, from ornate tail to gilded horn, she carried it everywhere atop its satin cushion inside a box of blue and white.

It remained safe there until it slipped out and shattered into five pieces on the kitchen floor. I found out that evening as we readied for our bedtime prayer. In my disappointed dad voice, I asked how she could let that happen, and she began to cry, saying, "I didn't mean to. I tried not to, but it just fell!"

I could tell it had broken her heart to see her little friend smashed to pieces, and tears filled her eyes as she asked me to fix it. I said something to her about it being an accident and it would be okay as I gently placed the box with the broken unicorn into her garbage bin. By morning, the box was back on the bureau, within arm's reach of Anna's bed. I told her that it wasn't safe to keep a box with shards of glass in it, so I took it again and placed it safely on Mommy's bureau until I could quietly dispose of it.

Knowing what it had meant to her, I set out to find a replacement but discovered that the store where it had been purchased had closed down. Luckily, I found something similar on eBay. I contacted the seller and told her about our situation. She was very touched by my daughter's story, saying that it reminded her of a similar experience she'd had during her own childhood. I made an offer and felt so relieved, excited, and appreciative when she accepted it.

When I received the unicorn in the mail, I waited secretly until bedtime. I went to Anna's bedside and told her there was a lady who had an orphan unicorn that needed a new home. I opened the box and I asked her, "Would you be willing to adopt it?"

Her eyes opened wide with wonder as she slowly exhaled, "Ohhh, whoooa." She picked it up so gently and said, "I wish I had show and tell so I could show it." I asked her if she liked it and she said, "I don't like it ... I love it! I'll never break this ever again." With that, her heart was healed and

I felt happy. As for her new friend, it only comes out every so often before it is tucked back into the box it came in, which may explain why unicorns are so seldom seen in our neck of the woods to this very day.

If you would like to make a donation
to St. Rita's building fund,
please contact us by phone at 780-524-3425
or by e-mail at stritavalleyview@gmail.com

ABOUT THE AUTHOR

Len Mac Lellan is a husband to Maureen and a father, teacher, and storyteller. Raised in Judique, Cape Breton, Nova Scotia and now raising his own children in Valleyview, Alberta, Mac Lellan has a strong sense of place and community. He takes great joy in his twenty-five years of teaching elementary students at St. Stephen's Catholic School, which is reflected in his being nominated for the 2006 Excellence in Teaching Award and receiving the Excellence in Catholic Education Award in 2012.

When not singing in the church choir or regaling his children – Alexis, Allan, and Anna – with his own stories, he is busy collecting natural and oral history so he can preserve the stories of others.

Proceeds from the sale of this book will be used to help pay for St. Rita's Gathering Centre in Valleyview, Alberta. Leonard is also the author of *God Will Provide*. This is his second book.